Claire Le Men

Translated by Jeffrey K. Butt

IF FLOWERS WERE LITTLE MONSTERS

A Field Guide to Fact and Fantasy

HELVETIQ publishing has been supported by the Swiss Federal Office of Culture with a structural grant for the years 2021–2025.

If Flowers Were Little Monsters
A Field Guide to Fact and Fantasy

Originally published as:
Monstres en fleurs
Un guide de botanique décalé

Text and illustrations: Claire Le Men
Translation from French: Jeffrey K. Butt
Typesetting and layout: Ewelina Proczko
Editor: Angela Wade
Proofreader: Danni Loe
Photogravure: Jean-Yves Mercy, Abers Studio

ISBN: 978-3-03964-036-2
First edition: March 2025
Printed in China

© 2025 HELVETIQ (SA)
Mittlere Strasse 4
CH-4056 Basel

TABLE OF CONTENTS

Camellia

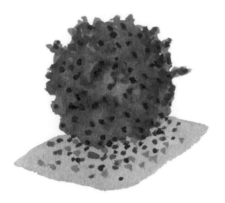

Just what is that big, round, green thing stomping its feet and leaving red marks everywhere?

It's a camellia! Camellias are shrubs that keep their thick, glossy, deep green leaves during winter, which is also when they bloom. And they do so abundantly! The shrub's full name is *Camellia japonica,* or Japanese camellia.

In Japanese, the word for camellia is *tsubaki,* meaning "tree with thick leaves." The eye-catching camellia flower doesn't lose its petals one by one; instead, they fall off all at once. So, for the ancient samurais, the camellia flower symbolized the fragility of life.

The camellia flower falls to the ground in one piece, like a brave samurai losing his head in battle.

The samurais even chose the camellia as their emblem. They were especially fond of a variety called Higo. Why? Because of its generous heart: more than 200 golden stamens surrounded by a ring, or corolla, of simple red petals.

With big, yellow, eye-like flowers, the Higo always has a look of surprise!

In Japan, people love single-flower camellias for their generous bouquet of stamens. But in China, flowers with showy stamens are considered loud and garish. The Chinese prefer double-flower camellias, which have several rows of petals.

The Europeans, too, have long been fascinated with double-flower camellias. In the 19th century, it was stylish for men to pin them to their lapel. The famous fashion designer Coco Chanel took note and, in the early 20th century, turned this accessory into one of her signature designs.

The camellia came to Europe quite by accident. It got confused with another species in the *Camellia* genus—one you might be familiar with... tea!

By the 17th century, the English had already developed a taste for tea. But tea was quite expensive because the tree from which it was made, *Camellia sinensis* (or "Chinese camellia"), was grown only in Asia. So, they ordered seeds from China to grow their own beloved tea leaves.

But instead of *Camellia sinensis,* they got *Camellia japonica*... Gag or gaffe, we'll never know!

The English would have to wait until the 18th century to grow their own tea. As luck would have it, British gardeners fell in love with the foliage and red flowers of *Camellia japonica*. And that's how all the different varieties we know today came to be.

If there were such a thing as a camellia monster, it would stomp around leaving red footprints all over the place. This MONSTRELLIA would have a big heart, with big, round, bewildered eyes to match.

Tough as a samurai, this Japanese creature would never be seen out of its green armor, not even to wash! Still, the mischievous MONSTRELLIA would take the occasional bath… if only to trick people into thinking it is its Chinese cousin who turns into tea when wet.

Mimosa

When the winter sun just isn't enough, mimosa flowers are there to brighten up the gloomy days from December to March.

It's truly quite amazing how the mimosa blooms in winter… and it's all because it thinks it's still in its native Australia. Down Under, the mimosa blooms in summer, which is winter in the Northern Hemisphere.

In the 18th century, the mimosa (sometimes called "silver wattle" or "blue wattle") embarked on a long journey northward. It adapted to its new environment, but if you check its passport, you'll see its real name is actually… acacia!

PASSPORT

Genus: ACACIA
Species: DEALBATA
Country of origin: AUSTRALIA
Alias: MIMOSA

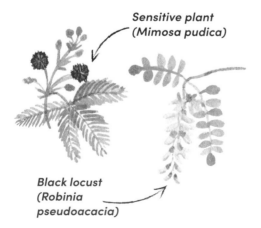

Sensitive plant (Mimosa pudica)

Black locust (Robinia pseudoacacia)

This plant's scientific name is *Acacia dealbata*. The true mimosa, *Mimosa pudica* (or "sensitive plant"), is an entirely different species, although it does resemble acacia with its pink pompom flowers. And the tree we call "acacia" is actually… black locust. How does anyone keep this stuff straight?

The word *dealbata* means "whitening" in Latin; as in the white coating (or pruinescence) that covers the mimosa. It's this coating that gives the pastel green mimosa leaves their pretty, pale silvery-green hue.

The frosty appearance of the mimosa is a result of that coating: a thin, waxy, slightly powdery skin that comes off when you rub it. You've probably already noticed it on some fruits, like plums and grapes.

This coating protects the plant from the elements, just like the sebum (or oil) on our own skin… but more flattering! While human skin can look greasy, mimosas are elegantly powdered. In fact, it's been said that mimosas have a sweet, powdery fragrance.

Mimosas are covered in flowers, all soft and fluffy, climbing over each other, as if trying to fly away. If only they had wings…

Like little, newly hatched chicks.

If mimosa flowers were monsters, there'd be tons of them, chirping away like baby chicks, climbing everywhere, jumping into the sky.

Everything about these MIMOMONSTERS would be warm and cuddly: from their down and smell to their cheerful winter colors.

Their cute little feet would be a pale silvery green and they'd be covered in baby powder, too; just like the kind we sprinkle on babies' bottoms to protect their skin.

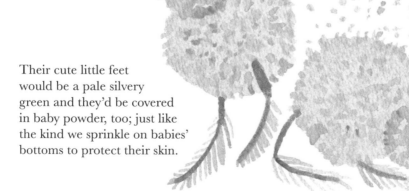

While MIMOMONSTERS are trying to fly away,
other flowers are digging their way out of the ground.

Hyacinth

In Greek mythology, Hyacinthus was a handsome young man… So handsome that two gods, Apollo and Zephyrus, fell in love with him. One day, Hyacinthus and Apollo were throwing a discus. Zephyrus grew jealous and blew a powerful wind, causing the discus to accidentally hit the beautiful boy in the head and kill him. From his blood emerged a flower: the hyacinth.

That spelled the end for poor Hyacinthus, but we have pretty flowers to remember him by: *Hyacinthus orientalis* (or "garden hyacinth").

With its bulbs poking through the soil, it's as though the hyacinth rises from the ground…

Or perhaps it's like a mole sticking its head out!

Interestingly, before opening, the hyacinth's flowers also look—quite oddly—like mole paws. Little hands with pink, shiny fingers—eeewww!

But it's the bluish-purple hyacinths that are the most popular. In fact, blue was their original color, before four centuries of selection and crossbreeding by humans.

In 18th-century Europe, people went crazy for hyacinths. Numerous varieties appeared and bulbs sold for astronomical prices. But they really took off thanks to the trendsetting Madame de Pompadour, a court favorite of King Louis XV of France. Today, we'd call her an "influencer."

Madame de Pompadour was such a fan of these heavily scented flowers that she had them planted all around the Palace of Versailles. It wasn't enough to admire them outside from March to May… No, she had to have indoor blossoms for winter, too! This was possible thanks to a practice known as "forcing," which involved the use of special vases.

This water-based growing technique is still used today to get hyacinths to bloom early, in December.

The hyacinth is all decked out in a green strapless dress and tightly curled, blue beehive hairdo. Does it remind you of a famous cartoon character?

If hyacinths were monsters, they'd live underground like moles. They'd also have tiny, pink—almost see-through—mole paws, with claws. Every now and then, they'd emerge from their tunnels to show off their striking hairdos.

HYAMONSTER heads would sometimes bear scratch marks from digging holes, but that's where the little flowers sprout from. Like moles, they would have poor eyesight, so the only way to find other HYAMONSTERS would be to sniff out their strongly scented curls.

Daffodil

With the wave of a magic wand, this flower makes spring appear.

When you start to see the daffodil, also known as narcissus, sometimes as early as February, you know it's soon time to wave goodbye to winter.

Using its megaphone-shaped corona, the daffodil broadcasts its message loud and clear: sun's out!

But winter still has a grip. So, the daffodil keeps its head and neck bundled up under a tiny scarf called a **spathe**, a stylish sheath from which the flower appears.

The befrilled, trumpet-headed daffodil literally toots its own horn! Just like the person it's named for, there's nothing shy about this plant. This narcissist knows it's the fairest of them all…

In Greek mythology, Narcissus was a young man of exceptional beauty. One day while drinking from a pool of water, he fell in love with his own reflection. He remained there, eyes glued to his own image, until he died… and then he turned into a flower. Like Narcissus the person, narcissus the plant stands at an angle, leaning toward the nearest source of water.

The daffodil is indeed a fatal beauty! All parts of the plant are poisonous for both humans and animals. The sap is also toxic to other plants, which is why you don't normally see daffodils in arrangements with other flowers. Daffodils need their own vase—no wonder they were once a symbol of arrogance and vanity.

The daffodil is like a snail, leaving behind a sticky, sappy trail that looks like egg whites.

And sometimes, the trumpet looks like the yolk…

And every now and then, it's an egg cooked sunny side up!

White or yellow, or even orangey or seashell-pink… perhaps, just perhaps, the daffodil chooses to look like an egg, so we know spring is just around the corner!

In spring, a variety known as "poet's daffodil" blankets damp meadows in a sea of white. A true miracle of nature!

In some countries, like the Netherlands and France, poet's daffodil is grown for its essential oils. Every spring, growers take to the fields to cut off millions of white flower heads with a giant comb-like device mounted on a wheel.

These daffodil heads are used to make perfume and are the last wildflowers still used in the fragrance industry. Farmers send the flowers to a local factory where the oil is extracted for perfume makers around the world!

The daffodil's scent is so complex and powerful that you could make a perfume from it alone. The famous French perfume maker Jean-Claude Ellena once said:

Few perfume oils smell like an entire countryside. Not only does the oil smell like the flower itself, but it also takes on the bitterness of the neighboring plants, the green of the meadow, the harshness of its surroundings, and if you've got a good nose, the stench of the animals. How can anyone say a smell isn't a place?

If the daffodil were a monster, it would usher in spring with a wave of its wand!

With its trumpet-like snout, the MONSTODIL would proudly proclaim: "Winter, winter, go away, it's now time for longer days! We want yellow everywhere, in our eggs and warm sunrays!" And all the other flowers would heed the gangly, yet charming, MONSTODIL's order to bloom.

Forget-me-not

In early spring, it's impossible not to notice this tiny, blue flower.

There's simply no forgetting the haunting gaze of the forget-me-not. People around the world must agree, because in German it's called *Vergissmeinnicht,* in Dutch *vergeet-mij-nietje,* in Spanish *nomeolvides*—which all mean "forget-me-not"—and so on, in Italian, Polish, Danish… and even Chinese!

The forget-me-not is blue in both senses of the word: as a symbol of eternal love, this sappy, sentimental little flower reminds forlorn lovers to remain forever true.

According to one legend, a knight was picking forget-me-nots for his beloved when he fell into water and drowned, weighed down by his armor. He had just enough time to toss her the bouquet and cry out, "Forget me not."

With their long, swaying arms, forget-me-nots always seem to be waving goodbye.

Another possible explanation for the flower's name is rooted in Greek mythology. Zeus thought he had given a name to every plant when a little flower cried out, "Don't forget me!" Zeus must have run out of ideas because he named it "forget-me-not."

He'd simply overlooked this little flower, smaller than a tiny mouse.

In fact, its scientific name, *myosotis,* means "mouse ear" in Greek. That's because the plant's fuzzy, round leaves look like mice ears.

Even its stem and little, bell-shaped buds are covered in a fluffy down. Everything about this pretty flower is small and delicate, just like a mouse.

If forget-me-nots were monsters, they'd be small and would have velvety ears. They'd be sentimental little things and defenders of true, eternal love. Naturally, people would call them FORGET-ME-NOMSTERS in all the languages of the world.

FORGET-ME-NOMSTERS would appear to lost lovers and, with a shake of their tail, remind them of their parting words… their piercing blue eyes a plea to stay forever true. With FORGET-ME-NOMSTERS, out of sight is never out of mind!

Iris

With its graceful lines, the iris rises tall and proud. There is something princely about the iris. No wonder the kings of France chose it as their emblem.

It all began with the first king, Clovis, who is said to have won a battle by hiding behind a thick clump of irises.

The kings that followed continued to use the iris flower as a symbol of victory; in fact, Louis VII put it on his royal arms. That's how *fleur de Louis* ("Louis' flower") became fleur-de-lis, a word used in English for the three-petaled iris flower associated with all things French. That's right, the same fleur-de-lis that graces the flag of Quebec, Canada.

The most popular irises are the ones that come in shades of blue. Their petals seem to change color, which is why they are described as iridescent or shimmering. In Greek mythology, Iris was a messenger who traveled on rainbows to bring news to the gods.

And the rainbow was the symbol chosen by Catherine de' Medici, the queen of France, who started the trend of wearing iris perfume. In paintings, she is often depicted with a large collar surrounding her head like the petals of her favorite flower.

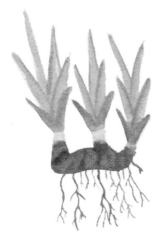

Today, irises are the most expensive ingredient in luxury perfumes, not because of the plant's royal origins, but the great care they require. To bring out the heavy, yet powdery and elegant tones, like those of the violet, the rhizome (or rootstalk) of the iris is dried for three years before the oils can be extracted.

It takes time for the iris to develop its scent. In fact, its flowers are not very fragrant at all. It's as though they've just woken up, lazing in an unmade bed.

With three droopy petals drifting back to sleep, the iris stretches out, like a graceful, lazy cat happily showing off its golden tail.

If the iris were a monster, it would spend all day lounging about. With an air of proud superiority, the regal MONSTIRIS would dilly-dally without a care in the world. It would linger in bed for hours before eventually rising to primp and preen: there's a nose to powder, shimmering clothes to don (don't forget the collar and rainbow scarf!), and a whiskery, golden tail to groom.

The MONSTIRIS would take three whole years to get ready, before finally dabbing on a delicate violet perfume. Then, off it would go to deliver its messages to the gods (nothing but good news, of course, like the return of fine weather), leaving a scented, rainbow trail in its wake.

What are all those
bright red spots?

Poppy

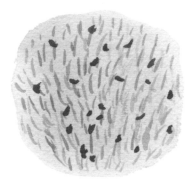

Small splatters of paint and spots so bright they seem almost surreal…

We must be talking about the poppy and its crinkled, delicate wings…

And big, curly lashes!

Don't the red petals look like a rooster's comb and wattle? The French must think so, because their word for poppy is *coquelicot*—a word that was originally an imitation of the rooster call *cocorico*, or "cock-a-doodle-doo" to us.

Certainly, the poppy has all the beauty of a bird. And like a bird, a poppy won't sit in your hand. Just pick one and watch the petals float away, like a bird taking wing…

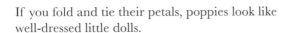

Or a butterfly that dies after being touched.

If you fold and tie their petals, poppies look like well-dressed little dolls.

But be extra careful or you might end up with a hairy stalk and a helmet head… or worse, a bowl cut!

If the poppy were a monster, it would come with butterfly wings, because poppies are as delicate as butterflies.

The POPMONSTER would be as striking as a bird, strutting its stuff like a rooster. This monster would try to act all tough in its helmet, but how could anyone be afraid of a monster with a bowl cut and long, loopy lashes?

Careful! The wings fall off when
you catch a POPMONSTER!

Acacia

A divine fragrance descends from high above our heads. We look up to see a tree that can grow to nearly 100 feet tall.

Just like the bees, we find its pretty clusters of flowers irresistible. We call it "acacia," but it's really the black locust, or false acacia.

A few pages back, we talked about the mimosa, or "true" acacia… But because the black locust can loosely pass for a member of the Acacia genus, its scientific name is *Robinia pseudoacacia*, or plain old "acacia" to most of us.

Ever heard of "black locust honey"? Probably not (sounds gross, right?!). But you might have heard of the nicer sounding "acacia honey." This honey is world-class, even if it is made from black locust trees.

Be careful, though! Behind its sweet, mild exterior…

Those little boot-shaped buds…

And those white caps that seem to give them all the innocence of a nun…

The acacia flower conceals a dangerous weapon: huge thorns!

If the acacia flower were a monster, it would crawl around like a millipede or caterpillar, each foot strapped into a little boot: a walking honey-flavored dessert!

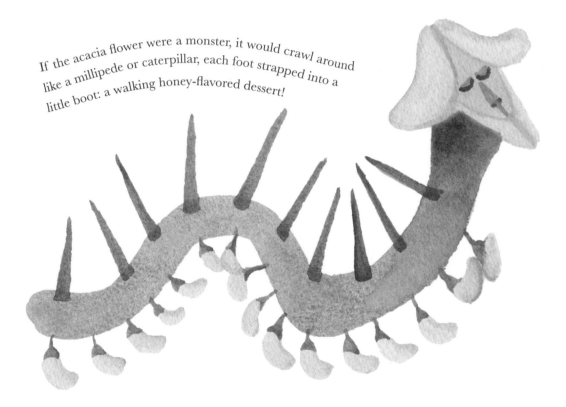

The MONSTRACIA would look innocent enough in its nun's cap, hands folded humbly in prayer. But its heavenly scent would lure prey, who'd meet their fate on those dreadful thorns lining its back!

Peony

The peony is a very shy flower. It hides away in its shell for days on end before finally daring to poke its head out.

Ever so cautiously it emerges… when our backs are turned! Like a wary hermit crab, the peony seems ready to whip back inside at the slightest sound.

A startled peony will blush, as peonies do. In the language of flowers (also known as floriography), the peony symbolizes shyness, sincerity, and shame.

Though meek and mild, the peony's peculiar shapes betray a flower with secrets to tell.

Deep within its heart lies a hidden deep-sea coral…

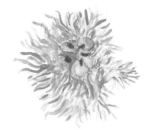

Where seaweed sways beneath the waves.

One moment, its fish-scale petals are neatly arranged…

The next, they're flapping, like a fin stirred by an invisible current. The peony loves to dance and prance, like a ballerina in her tutu!

Even its wavy, deeply lobed leaves look like the fins of an exotic fish from the Far East, which is where the peony is from. In China, the peony is the "queen of flowers!"

For around 2,500 years, the Chinese have practically worshipped the peony for both its beauty and its many healing properties.

If the peony could be a monster, it would be an extremely bashful one. It would appear when no one was looking, and if anyone saw it, it would immediately turn red. The PEONSTER would make its home deep in the sea, hidden among the corals and seaweed.

It wouldn't have a mouth: to stop it from telling its many medicinal secrets. With its ruffled tail fluke and dancing side fins, it would glide through the water with all the grace of a ballerina. Like the flower it's named after, the PEONSTER would be from Asia, where people would give it the royal treatment!

While the blushing PEONSTER prefers to swim in the depths of the sea, far away from all eyes, there's another Monster Flower that actually likes the company of people...

Elderberry

Elderberries love to be around people and are a very common garden bush. They certainly aren't fussy, as they readily grow in disturbed soil and at abandoned sites.

Elderberries are great to have around because they can do just about anything. To start, they have many therapeutic properties. And their white, fragrant flowers are used to make a tasty syrup, elderberry champagne, and other delicious treats.

The berries are so black that in addition to jams, they are used to make dyes and inks—hence, the scientific name *Sambucus nigra* (*nigra* meaning "black" in Latin).

It is believed that *sambucus* comes from the Ancient Greek word *sambúkē,* meaning "harp" or "flute." In fact, elderberry wood is hollow and naturally soft, so it's great for making magic flutes and other musical instruments.

Elderberry leaves have uneven edges, like feathers, and smell rather bad, but they make excellent garden compost.

Clearly, elderberries are ideal shrubs: so ideal, you might just want to marry one! In fact, their tiny flowers look like elegant lace, or a fine wedding veil, maybe even a lovely wedding gown…

Or a dragonfly wing.

Each tiny, white elderberry flower has five stamens capped with a ball of cream-colored pollen. Don't they look a bit like snails' eyes?

Elderberry flowers also have something in common with wedding doves.

Perhaps all this is why Prince Harry requested an elderberry wedding cake, with elderberry syrup from the Queen's Garden, of course! The cake cost (gulp) over $50,000!

Harry & Meghan's wedding cake

- 200 Italian lemons
- 500 organic Suffolk eggs
- 20 kg of butter
- 20 kg of flour
- 20 kg of sugar
- 10 bottles of elderberry syrup from Sandringham House

If elderberries were monsters, brides and grooms would get them as wedding gifts, just so they could watch one majestically fly away. Though wild and free, ELDERMONSTERS would enjoy being around people. Despite having panoramic vision thanks to those five snail eyes crowning their heads, ELDERMONSTERS wouldn't be hard to catch!

ELDERMONSTER tears would be collected to make an excellent ink, while their poop would be harvested and turned into a rich manure. Their sweet saliva would be used to make exquisite royal wedding cakes and the songs from their magic flutes would be simply spellbinding!

Clover

It's easy to overlook these poor little plants amid the chaos of an overgrown roadside. We just walk all over them, like a car accidentally running over a furry critter…

Clover is so small and plentiful that we barely notice it. But if you give it a closer look, you'll see just how pretty it truly is.

A clover flower looks like it just stepped out of the beauty salon—with highlights and spiky, gelled hair.

The little clover is an excellent source of protein for large grazing animals. It's what we call a "fodder plant."

Bees love clover, too, for making their honey, so it's also considered a "bee plant."

Sadly, clover gets no respect. Instead, we step on it, walk on it, trample it. Why? Because it's simply too common. This hardy, resilient plant grows everywhere, so people don't appreciate it.

Except when it comes with four leaves! The four-leaf clover is so rare, people spend hours combing through the grass to find one!

If there were such thing as a clover monster—a CLOGRE—it would be no bigger than the bees we also ignore buzzing around in the grass. Not only would CLOGRES have to watch out for careless feet, they'd also be hapless meals for hungry cows, sheep and goats.

Once common and widespread, they would be an endangered species… In some places, people would poach them in hopes of finding the rare four-toed CLOGRE that is said to bring good luck.

The lowly clover gets no more love than
the grass growing around it!

Cows like it for its sweetness (you could
consider it "cow candy") but, to us,
clover is plain, old, off-color grass, and
not a plant with a pretty flower… The
exact opposite of the buttercup, which
everyone loves for its buttery yellow
color, even if it is poisonous…

Buttercup

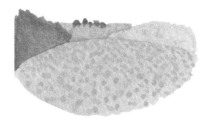

Clad in sparkling gold, this flower is *definitely* the prettiest weed there is.

If the buttercup gleams like… well… butter, it's to better attract insects. In fact, buttercup is covered in a glossy film resembling drops of nectar, which pollinators find appealing. When it comes to reproduction, this plant holds nothing back!

Some species of buttercup, like creeping buttercup, spread thanks to their **stolons**, or runners, that sprout new stems.

Buttercup grows in tight packs that aren't at all afraid of the lawn mower. It might look delicate, but buttercup is so hardy, it's considered invasive.

Cows keep their distance because they know buttercup is poisonous. This allows the plant to keep spreading from field to field without any danger of being eaten.

Who would have guessed a buttery little flower could be poisonous? Buttercup looks innocent enough with those five round petals; so simple even a child could draw it…

Even mature buttercup flowers look young, thanks to the thin mustache growing around their mouths.

Buttercup is the classic teenager: neither man nor boy, oily skin, vigorous, and with a peach-fuzz mustache… cute but certainly not without toxic traits…

Buttercup acts all mighty with its lanky, string-bean frame, but look it in the face and you'll know it's just a little squirt!

If buttercups were monsters, they would breed like rabbits. These eternal teens would move around in packs, looking spiffy, but usually up to no good and nonsense.

With peach-fuzz whiskers sprouting around their snouts, BUTTERMONSTERS would act tough, but how could anyone take them seriously with those little round, buttery pompoms on their butts?

Dandelion

If there was ever a flower with a double identity, this is it! A sun that becomes a clock!

They're sometimes called "pee-the-beds" because they're a diuretic—in plain English, they make you pee!

We're talking about the dandelion. "Dandelion" was taken from the French *dent-de-lion*, meaning "lion's tooth"—a reference to the plant's jagged, or toothed, leaves.

Other languages did the same: *dente di leone* in Italian, *Löwenzahn* in German, and so on in Spanish, Danish, Romanian, and other languages.

It's certainly easy to see something resembling a
lion's mane in a dandelion flower…

And the fleecy softness of an old lion's fur.

And when you blow on the seedhead, or
"dandelion clock," to make a wish, all that's left
is a small, round muzzle.

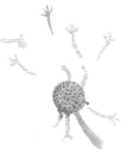

And the large buds at the end of the stem look
like a lion's tail.

Dandelion is often confused with other similar-
looking yellow flowers, like cat's ear (or "false
dandelion"), which has leaves covered in prickly
hairs, like a small cactus. Fortunately, both
species are edible.

The dandelion is a common graveyard plant
because it grows well in disturbed soil. So, after
a burial, it is often the first plant to take root.

If dandelion monsters existed,
they would pee all over the place,
especially in bed!

Young DANDEMONSTERS
would sport a beautiful, yellow
mane, which would turn grey as
they aged, along with their beard,
just below their two lion fangs.

Before dying, their once-pristine manes
would be wispy and thin, like the hair on our
heads, and blow away with the wind. If you
see a DANDEMONSTER shedding its
fur, make a wish, quick! It will come true!

The life cycle of a DANDEMONSTER

To give birth, DANDEMONSTERS camp out in cemeteries. There, they take root on graves to enjoy the peaceful, quiet company of the dearly departed.

A teenager with its flashy mane.

An aging adult specimen shedding its white mane.

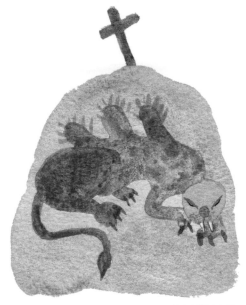

A bald, elderly DANDEMONSTER returns to the same grave where it was born.

Honeysuckle

Honeysuckle is a vine or shrub from the *Caprifoliaceae* family. This term is made up of the Latin words *capra,* meaning "goat," and *folium,* meaning "leaf." Indeed, honeysuckle is quite good at climbing; just like a goat.

Or perhaps the name has something to do with the many animals, such as deer, that love to feed on young sprouts and suckle from the plant's honey-sweet flowers.

"Intoxicating" is one word that has been used to describe the aroma of honeysuckle. In fact, honeysuckle itself seems a little drunk, with vines rambling off in every direction, and never in a straight line…

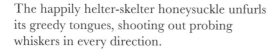

Or it's a cavorting kid. There's something in the devilish grin and oddly rectangular eyes of a young goat that resemble the frenzied behavior of honeysuckle.

The happily helter-skelter honeysuckle unfurls its greedy tongues, shooting out probing whiskers in every direction.

And its petals splay to reveal five fingers… Four point downward, except the middle going in the other direction… like a bad-mannered lout flipping us the bird!

If honeysuckle were a monster, it would usually be intoxicated, drunk on its own heady scent. The HONEYMUCKLE would jump up on everything, just like a young goat and every bit as crazy and mischievous…

an endless, fumbling pursuit of fun and folly, tongue stuck out, tail and whiskers spiraling in every direction. No point trying to tame the impish, little HONEYMUCKLE beast— this kid would just keep on "kidding" around.

Lavender

From late June to mid-August, this "plant with a thousand virtues," as it is known, paints the landscape a magical blue.

Lavender grows best in arid, rocky soil. Like a cat, it doesn't like water and loves to bask in the summer sun.

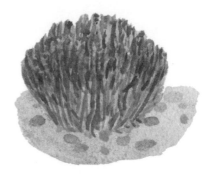

Lavender is well-suited to the climate of southern France where you'll find endless fields with alternating lines of ocher and purple. Tourists from all over the world flock to the Provence region to snap photos of this "blue gold."

These lines are just like the stripes on all those bees that go mad for lavender nectar (which makes an excellent honey).

But more than honey, lavender is grown for something else: its famous essential oil, which smells wonderful, has healing properties, and can prevent infections by killing bacteria.

Lavender tea is soothing and is great for getting a good night's sleep. In fact, if a calm, gentle night had a smell, it would be lavender.

Lavender is also the smell of clean sheets. "Lavender" comes from the Latin *lavare*, meaning "to wash" or "purify." No surprise that "laundry" comes from the same Latin root, since lavender has long been used to make linens smell clean and fresh.

The Ancient Romans used lavender to add fragrance to their bath water, protect their linens, and disinfect their thermal baths.

Even today, people store pouches of dried lavender with their clothes to keep them smelling fresh and protect them from moths.

If lavender were
a monster, it would be
like a sleepy cat savoring
the summer heat on a
stone terrace. To behold
a LAVENDOGRE
would be pure
bliss.

Like the purr of a pussy cat, its mere presence would wash all our troubles away. LAVENDOGRES would always smell fresh because, just like cats, they'd spend all day licking themselves clean… That is, when not curled up and fast asleep on a bed or in a linen closet.

LAVENDOGRES make terrific pets. Here are some reasons to adopt one:

A soothing, calming presence

A wonderful scent to keep your clothes smelling fresh

A healing saliva for fixing booboos

Keeps moths away

It only needs a little, sunny corner to thrive

I take up waaay less space than that flower!

Sunflower

The sunflower is a huge flower that reaches for the sun and can grow to 13 feet tall!

The sunflower is as big as an elephant, with stump-like feet, too…

Or is it more like a giraffe? Look at all those colored spots.

In its youth, when still just a green bud, the sunflower is hairy and clawed. At that stage, its head follows the movement of the sun, as the name suggests.

But when the flower opens up, the sunflower stops turning and faces only the rising sun: the ideal position for catching the sun's first rays and attracting pollinators.

It takes A LOT of insects to pollinate all those flowers so we can enjoy the fruit we call… sunflower seeds! Humans have been growing sunflowers for 4,000 years just for the sunflower seeds and the oil they produce.

Gently, the sunflower takes a peek, revealing its spellbinding patterns.

The spiral patterns radiating from its heart are the true flowers of the sunflower. As for the yellow petals that look like sunrays, well those aren't petals at all, but "ray flowers."

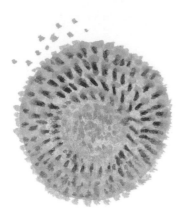

The sunflower spits pollen from the tip of its many tubular flowers, which look like little protruding tongues…

Coating everything around it in gold dust and sunshine.

Together, all these little flowers will eventually produce seeds arranged in an incredible spiral of geometric perfection. They are perfectly spaced, based on a mathematical equation known as the "golden ratio."

To come up with such a design, the sunflower must be a math whiz! By using the golden ratio, the sunflower ensures its "inflorescence"—a big word for all those little flowers at the center—contains the greatest number of seeds possible.

If sunflowers were monsters, their first order of business would be to find the sun, using their long giraffe necks to swing their giraffe heads from east to west. Then, these SUNMONSTERS would soak up the sun's first rays with their golden manes. They'd gleefully bask in the warmth, while spitting golden glitter from the tip of their tongues.

SUNMONSTERS would have more than just good looks on their side— they'd be smart, too, using their math and geometry skills to find perfection and harmony. And with all that squinting from staring at the sun, they would cry sunflower-oil tears—a gift for humankind.

Nasturtium

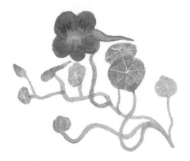

With their climbing vine-like stems, nasturtiums spread quite easily, like water lilies… but on land.

Those pretty, round leaves make nasturtiums look wide-eyed with bewilderment…

Or perhaps they're a multitude of suction-cup feet that help the plant crawl and climb everywhere?

We once called this plant "Indian cress" because its edible leaves taste like another plant: watercress.

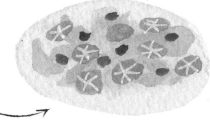

Nasturtiums are a tasty addition to any salad.

Other languages named nasturtiums after the long **spurs** in their flowers that look like hoods, such as those worn by Capuchin monks; for example, in French they're called *capucine* and in Spanish *capuchina*.

But nasturtiums, with their popping yellow and orange colors, don't really resemble the somber, brown clothes worn by those charitable monks.

Clanging together their big, noisy cymbals…

Bursting with blooms until deep into autumn, when the first frost strikes…

Always sporting that big, gap-toothed grin…

Nasturtiums are made for eating! Their flowers and leaves are jam-packed with vitamin C!

If nasturtium monsters existed, they'd always be up for a good time—nothing monkish about these plants!

These gap-toothed, boundlessly energetic, cymbal-clanging, cheery MONSTERTIUMS would literally be climbing the walls, thanks to their suction-cup feet!

Japanese anemone

This light and delicate flower waves back and forth, ever so gracefully, in the autumn breezes.

Anemones owe their name to their feathery seeds that can travel vast distances on the gentlest of winds (*anemos* means "wind" in Greek).

It's hard not to be smitten with those green eyes surrounded by long, yellow, fluffy lashes… In Greek mythology, Anemone was a "nymph," or spirit of nature. After Zephyrus, God of the Wind, fell in love with her, Anemone's husband grew jealous and turned her into a flower (of course, the same fate often befell Zephyrus' lovers… remember Hyacinth?).

True to their name, Japanese anemones owe their elegance to their simplicity. They come in white or pastel pink and are the most famous and sophisticated of all anemones.

The Japanese anemone could almost pass for an oriental wading bird, standing tall on long, slender legs, poised to take flight.

But with a head too big for its body, it's more like a defenseless little bird. Because it belongs to the *Ranunculus* family, it's shaped like a buttercup, with simple, round petals—again, like a child might draw!

If a Japanese anemone were a monster,
it would have a slender build, with wings,
big wading-bird feet, and a head that
bobs in the wind.

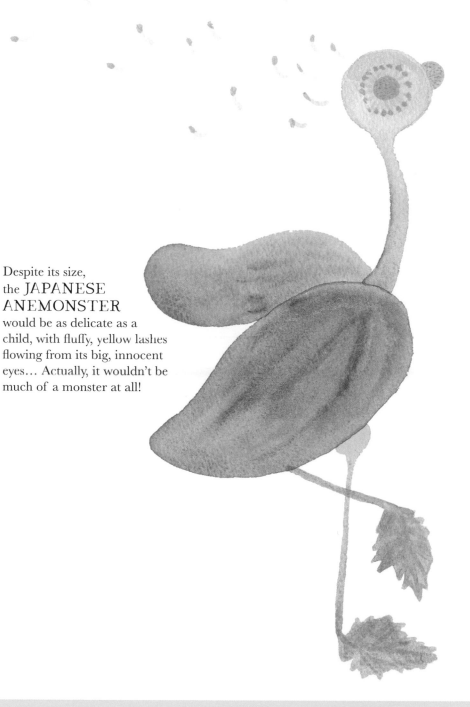

Despite its size,
the JAPANESE
ANEMONSTER
would be as delicate as a
child, with fluffy, yellow lashes
flowing from its big, innocent
eyes... Actually, it wouldn't be
much of a monster at all!

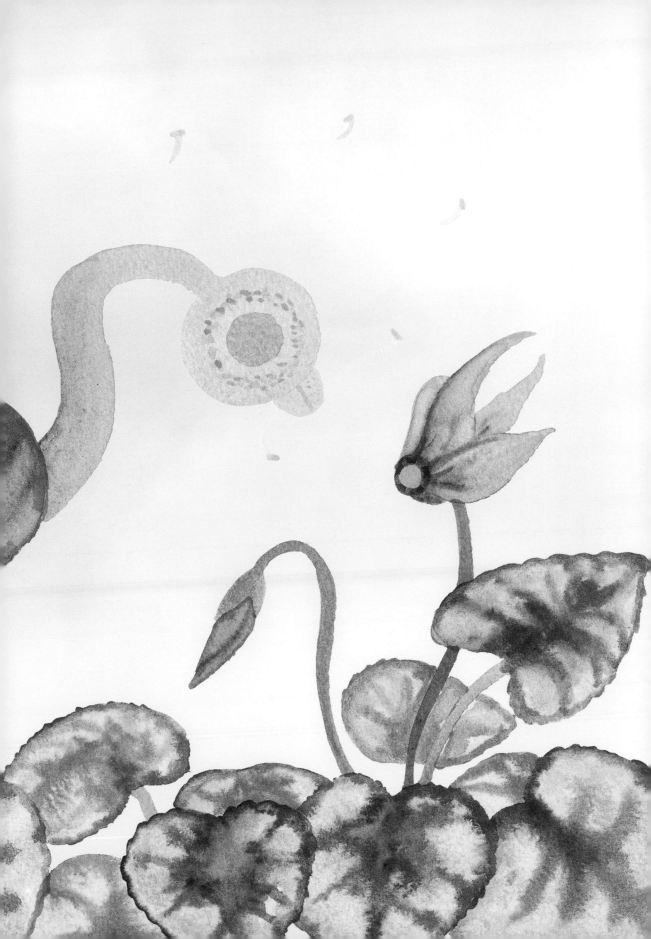

Cyclamen

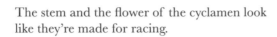

The stem and the flower of the cyclamen look like they're made for racing.

A powerful engine carving a path through sky and sea. You'd think aerodynamic engineers had something to do with the design of their propeller-shaped petals.

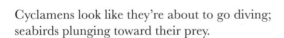

Safety first, though! Check out the tiny, built-in life preserver.

Cyclamens look like they're about to go diving; seabirds plunging toward their prey.

The flower buds look poised to attack, too, with their petals puckered into a sharp beak.

The dark green leaves of the ivy-leaved cyclamen give the plant its name—they look like ivy leaves… or maybe little dragon wings!

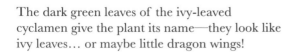

Ivy-leaved cyclamens *(Cyclamen hederifolium)* are very adaptable and are the easiest species of cyclamen to grow in the garden. They might be small, but these shade-loving plants require very little care and can live for a long time.

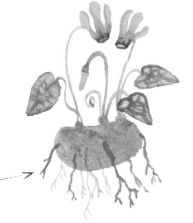

Some live to be a hundred years old and can have an enormous **tuber**, an underground organ for storing nutrients, weighing more than 30 pounds!

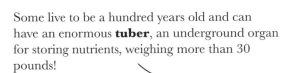

In fact, the cyclamen, which means "circle" in Greek, owes its name to those round, bread-shaped tubers.

These tubers contain a toxic substance, the similarly named cyclamin, so it's best not to put this "bread" anywhere near your mouth!

You'd be forgiven for assuming the "circle" name had to do with the cyclamen's unusual behavior: after blooming, the seed-bearing peduncle, or flower stem, begins to curl at the tip and keeps coiling until it reaches the ground.

Cyclamens are a symbol of beauty in the language of flowers. So, if someone gives you a cyclamen plant, it could be a sign of true love… or a display of jealousy.

If the ivy-leaved cyclamen were a monster, it would be quite beautiful thanks to its long, stylishly coiled tail.

But don't be fooled by the petiteness of the pretty CYCLAMONSTER— not only would it be jealous, but aggressive, too. It would glide through the air on its little dragon wings. Suddenly, it would spiral downward to catch its prey with frightening speed; its beak slicing through the air and then the water.

But the CYCLAMONSTER would never have to worry about drowning, thanks to the little life preserver wrapped around its head!

Dahlia

The dahlia is native to Central America, where the Aztecs called it *cocoxochitl*, meaning "water cane," because of its hollow stem.

The Aztecs ate the bulbous dahlia roots; so it was introduced to Europe in the 19th century as a plant for food.

Little bead-shaped buds

But the dahlia tuber's trip to Europe did not have the same success as the potato. People found it too bitter, despite tasting like an artichoke. It was a different story, though, for the dahlia flower, which lasts until first frost. Gardeners were love-struck!

Across Europe, people began to crossbreed dahlias, giving rise to hybrids with spectacular flowers. Today, there are over 57,000 varieties! The dahlia is the most diverse plant when it comes to color and structure: it now comes in every size, shade, and shape imaginable! Its petals can be round or wispy or curly; its colors can be solid or spotted or striped; and the blooms can be laid out in single or multiple rows…

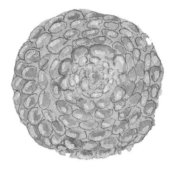

The dahlia is beautiful and glamorous! Sometimes it wears its hair up, like the pompom or ball dahlia…

Sometimes it goes for the layered look of the collarette dahlia…

And other times, it has spiky hair, like the cactus dahlia…

And just like a tropical bird, dahlias come in every bright color you can think of!

That is… every color but blue.
In 1846, the Royal Caledonian Horticultural Society in Edinburgh, Scotland, offered a cash prize of 2,000 pounds to the first person to grow a bluc dahlia… a fcat that no onc has cvcr managed, even to this very day!

If there were a dahlia monster, it would be true to its roots and wear Aztec clothing. Its bright parrot colors would give it a festive air. There'd be a crest of spiky hair sprouting from the MONSTRAHLIA's pompom head, and it would have a hollow stalk for a beak and beady little eyes!

Or maybe, just maybe, it would be blue. As an imaginary creature, the **MONSTRAHLIA** could be that one color—among all the varieties there are—that has eluded us… because with monsters, anything is possible!

Claire Le Men

Claire Le Men fell in love with flowers during the COVID-19 pandemic. Since she likes to take a closer look at things and has a fertile imagination, she quickly discovered there were monsters hiding behind a flower's pretty colors and innocent appearance. Claire Le Men lives in Brittany, France, and is the author of several graphic novels, one autobiographical graphic essay, and one novel. *If Flowers Were Little Monsters* is her first children's book.

How to make your very own Monster Flower

You can create your own Monster Flower in three easy steps: look, learn, and imagine. You're the one who gets to decide what your monster will be! And because monsters are imaginary, there's no right or wrong way to do it... If anything, the more monstrous you make it, the better!

1) Look

a. Flowers are found everywhere, and all year long, too! Look around and pick one.

b. Does your flower remind you of anything? An animal? Does it look shy? Proud? Does it seem happy? Wise? Is it big? Small? The possibilities are endless!

c. Take a step back and have a look. Is the flower growing in a tree or on a shrub or bush? Or is it sprouting right out of the ground? Is it growing all by itself, or are there others? Does it creep or climb?

d. Now take a closer look. Turn it around to see it from all sides and angles. How would you describe its petals, leaves, and stem? How about its shape, color, and texture, and so on? Is it smooth or fuzzy? Shiny or spiky? Can you see any roots or seeds?

e. Keep an eye on how your flower changes. Does it look different at different times? How does it look when its petals are open? What happens as it starts to wilt and wither? Does it change color? Can you see any fruit?

f. There may be other things you notice, too. Does the flower have a special scent? Is it rare or common?

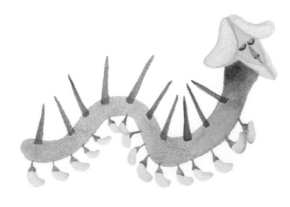

2) Learn

a. What's the name of your flower? Plants have both a scientific name in Latin and a common name. Some also have "folk" names that may vary from place to place. Look up your plant in a dictionary to learn the etymology, or origin, of its name. You can learn a lot about a flower this way.

b. What time of the year does your plant bloom? And what kind of climate does it need? Does it grow in shade or full sun? How much water does it require?

c. Where does the flower come from? Has it been adopted by a region or country as its official flower?

d. Are there any legends or myths surrounding the flower's history? Is the flower depicted in artwork or used in a common saying?

e. Does it have any special symbolic meaning? That often depends on the country. Is the flower associated with any special occasions?

f. Does it have any special qualities? Is it a medicinal or healing plant? Is it used to make perfume? How about honey? Is it edible or poisonous?

3) Imagine

a. Now that you've looked and learned, you can start to imagine what your flower would look like if it were a monster. Use your knowledge, observations, and creativity to tell your Monster Flower's story. What will you call it? One option is to combine the flower's name with a word like "monster" or "ogre."

b. Draw a picture of your Monster Flower. You can have a lot of fun weaving the plant's features into your flower's story.

c. Remember—with monsters, anything is possible! They can be any shape you want. They can look like a real animal or have all the colors of the rainbow. Maybe they have wings… or a tail… or claws… or multiple eyes!

d. You don't have to figure out who or what your monster is on the first try… In fact, your monster might even have a few surprises in store for you! By mixing all these things together, your monster will take shape all by itself, almost as if it existed all along and was just waiting for you to find it…